BONE SENSE

BONE SENSE

LAURIE LYNN MUIRHEAD

thistledown press

Thistledown Press Ltd.
118 - 20th Street West
Saskatoon, Saskatchewan, S7M 0W6
www.thistledownpress.com

Library and Archives Canada Cataloguing in Publication

Muirhead, Laurie Lynn
Bone sense / Laurie Lynn Muirhead.

Poems.
ISBN 978-1-927068-07-6

I. Title.

PS8626.U375B66 2012 C811'.6 C2012-904721-X

Cover and book design by Jackie Forrie
Printed and bound in Canada

Canada Council for the Arts / Conseil des Arts du Canada
Saskatchewan Arts Board
Canadian Heritage / Patrimoine canadien

Thistledown Press gratefully acknowledges the financial assistance of the Canada Council for the Arts, the Saskatchewan Arts Board, and the Government of Canada through the Canada Book Fund for its publishing program.

Acknowledgements

This book would not exist without the encouragement and support of Lynda Monahan. Her poetic beauty and wisdom have been a solid foundation for this project. Also, thank you to the members of sans nom poetry group, Veryl, Carla, Jan and Beth. Your friendship, respect and honesty especially when it comes to critiquing are invaluable.

A great deal of gratitude goes out to Thistledown Press for giving these poems a set of wings and to my editor Susan Musgrave for honing their ability to fly. It has been an absolute delight and honour working with such a proficient team.

I wish to thank the editors of *The New Quarterly*, *Transition* and CBC Radio (Kelley-Jo Burke) for showcasing my work along with the local coffee houses that gave the poems a voice.

And to my family, thank you for your unwavering support, love and patience. Your character, wit and charm will always be a source of inspiration.

"O farmers excessively fortunate, if only they recognized their blessings!" (page 62) is a quote from Virgil Georgics ii, 458.

CONTENTS

Anchored

Holding On

For

Ward, Justin, Casey

now and forever

Bone Sense

Something is stirring
in the garden, perennials
ornamental rosebush
like green leaves
just before a storm
small shudder then shake
bone sense

Perhaps prairie wool
under my skin
dry-grass words breathe willow
song of thistle, family, farm

Perhaps your laundry
out on the line
mended jeans, tired socks
wind-whipped cotton
thread bare, who?
naked truth bleeds

Small Coyote

Born my father's daughter
bake pies, wash clothes, dry dishes, *not I*
pulled on barn boots and chore clothes
slipped out the back porch, shadowed
his footsteps, pillar of silence allowed me the tailings
three posts and a four by four, *stay back!*
only — when his world was right
bales stacked, potatoes dug, harvest bone-dry
in the bin — would he allow me to press into his space
secure a double knot on the hooves of hard labour
hold the tape measure, *pull tight!*
squaring poles for a barn . . . and only
when he'd suddenly erupt, in the case of
hellish weather, wild stock or blown gaskets
would I run for the bush, small coyote
tight into the shadows, wait for the smoke to clear

Never a Good Mix

Your Side of the Fence

When I saw you
at the 4-H bingo
tight blue wranglers
cowboy boots
tarnished brown
straw hat down
wavy hair wild
shy smile, *I knew*

You were the one
took me to A&W
weekend rodeos
small town fairs
loved me more
than your '79 ford

Bought Boulet boots
women's wranglers
low wheeling spurs
up into the saddle
tossed me a rope, *let's treat*
pink-eye, foot rot, pneumonia

Nothing short of impossible
made me see women
from your side of the fence

Midnight Witness

At midnight, I bundle up
my turn to check
the black-baldy cows chewing cud
grunt in discomfort
they know me and lie still
breathing ghostly into frigid air
against the light of my lantern

Old Ginger, she ignores me
glassy eyes in the darkness
The crook in her tail, udder tight
tells me she will give birth soon

So I wait, just as you would
perched on the wooden fence
in this open air stadium, cold and tired
unable to sort through my thoughts
of how I married the farm
how two hundred cows calving in January
were not in the agreement

Aurora borealis dances her distraction
spills colour into a coyote's sadness
Even he knows I am nothing more
than a midnight witness to new life
that shivers in the night

Slow Silence

She lies on a barren field
both hips stifled, tiny quivers against her drum
you and I argue, *what about this damn cow*
she'll never get up

As always, I refuse common sense
pack your words into barley straw beneath her belly
feed her oats, second-cut alfalfa
induce her at midnight
try to save the calves

That night she and I, frozen field into bone
close to her body, swallowed in self pity
why can't I leave? let you shoot her
after all she's just a cow, easily replaced
but I can't, and I won't, without one ounce of try
here to the end

Three bitter nights, thirty below, slow silence
slivers of ice intimidate, *don't lose faith*
my hoping on hope for one small miracle
this damn cow will get up

Somewhere between cold and tired your words
fall heavy, ashen fog and coyotes close in
long shadows howl hunger, they know and wait
for one of us to die

All Borders Closed

Early evening, January's bite
scours the barnyard, cold bones
winter breath everywhere, unwanted

The kuvian dog marks his territory
leaves me to check, any sign of birthing

Coyotes cackle, trio of boredom
looking for the dog, teasing
come on coward, come out
let's play do or die

Perhaps they'll kill, cross his border
sly around new born flesh
wait for the opportunity

Patience is the coyote, his game
mama cow off guard
warm blood spills liquid stars

Not this night, the dog, too smart
marks again and returns
all borders closed

The coyotes retreat, slide north
three thieves in a shifting wind
curled into moonlight, they dream
the dog, his borders . . . hunger

A Good Question

Why do we have cows?
we curse their cost, they're hard to chase
we fight, throw sticks
run wild, *cut her off at the gate*
which gate?
that gate
there's three gates
you know the one, just do it
I walk away — *you're on your own*
curse and sweat and chase

Why do we have cows?
this cold calving, up all winter
when others hibernate, we freeze
pulling life from womb into that barn
he's cold
I know he's cold, got him in time
let's quit January do April
make a great bull don't you think?
I think we're crazy
get him nursing, I'll check the rest

Her teats, my hands chapped
lathered in udder balm
cold muzzle up into her breast
he suckles, shivers then sleeps

I ask, "why do we have cows?"
You say, "that's a good question"

Only Trying

We strode two abreast, frozen breath
hockey sticks in hand, no blade
ends frayed, poised to strike

There she stood fired eyes fixed, enraged
pawing up a storm, devoted guardian
her premature calf

Your strategy, simple
whack the cow, grab the calf and run

Not that easy, her bluff was huge
so was she, through snowstorm of straw
blizzard of words, you swung, I missed
she charged, I ran

Wish she could have understood
only trying to help

Did you know the help is getting tired
tired of being chased, yelled at
cursed out

Should have stood your ground, called her bluff
that's all you ever say

Your bluff, my ground, I'm standing it now
really won't mess with another of these cows

Transformation

Return from work, greetings!
my step full of rubber boots and bones
remnants of calving woes
cow crap thaw and sour silage

Annoyed with these bones, the smell
dirty dog barricade, *get!*
quick dodge and dart
through the door, throw my bags
and change, from slacks to sweats
settle into a cup of strong black tea
raw woollen sweater and yesterday's socks

Return to slop and slush, wild goose sky
check for new birth and sick calves
chase, tackle and treat
spring scours and bronchial pneumonia

Bones have a memory of their own
this farm feels good

Coyote

I watch you . . . travel the hill-side
back and forth, back and forth
nose to ground, boundaries and food

You're a shifty fellow
eager for a change of wind
mark territory, disappear

I've watched you for three days now
much too close to the herd
your uneasiness worries me into light slumber
calls me to attention just before midnight

I warned you coyote, threatened you
with your very life at the first sign of blood
there are plenty of spring gophers to eat

Not my meat, coyote!

We'll leave you alone . . . only
if you play fair

But you don't, you hurl insults at the
wide-eyed moon, flesh, blood and stars
you kill the weak one, *coward*

And the men are in a frenzy
take the rifle, it's the big blond one
he's trouble, leave the female and her pups
get the male

And I can't go for the kill
tend a fretted mama cow, her half-eaten calf
try to make sense of life and death, *what's fair?*

The shot is clean . . . lethal
and I concede there are no winners in this field
we've both sustained losses
perhaps . . . we can just call it square

Ambushed

Pussy willows and overhead honkers
gophers hungry poking up through their holes
all of us ambushed, unexpected blizzard

With wet snow came more work
two hundred baby calves
huddling in the willows, damp bodies
my fingers and toes cold

So I spread bales of barley straw
aching hours of push and shove
wonder why we work against nature
don't calve the early summer season
but I've wondered this for twenty years now
and nothing has changed

only when I burn these rubber boots and
toss my pitchfork will things be different

Rare Breed
(for Bob)

Like little boys with red wagons
they show up in the spring
in search of bloodlines
small at birth, strong in calving ease

Barter for price
need at least two more bulls than last year
insist on semen test, full guarantee

Deal or no deal, they sit at my table
in faded denim, leathered skin, bloodshot eye
hungry for chit-chat, black coffee
the oatmeal cake made two days ago

Tell tales of weary nights pulling calves
backwards, sideways, tail first
with a leg down, too - damn - big

Curse weather and politicians
price of a new four by four
laugh about the wife being chased
the stupid brown dog blind in one eye
who refuses to quit

Suddenly dusk
should have made trail long before now
they grab Stetsons, more cake and leave
with a cowboy's call on wisdom
it's been a bloody hard spring
mud up to our bellies for months
this year, only strong calves and good women
will survive

Never a Good Mix

Today we brand together in silence
agreement forged through experience
wife husband cows, never a good mix

Air thick with smoke, burnt hair
charred flesh, you curse
weary with the day, angry just because

Your cranky knuckles grab hot irons
that crackle, spit hot, scald skin
no time for pain, head-gate clangs and bangs
as iron tracks in winter
another calf restrained in steel
left hip scorched, R-lazy-S

Mamma cows bellow, they pace
pride of barnyard lioness
fury in their eyes, anxiety under skin
chars any good bone of humour
only when our blistered spirits heal
will the silence between us   end

Talk Dirt

Every morning at eight
I take the same trail as the cows
down to the dugout, check water
talk dirt, whine about the weather
worry about my children
wonder about this farm

worry about my children
wonder about fuel prices

worry about my children
wonder about feed stocks

Should I take another path
perhaps through the hayfield
via groves of black poplar
shadowed thoughts, storm clouds
what about the weather
worry about the feed

what about the weather
worry about cattle prices

what about the weather
worry about the U.S. dollar

This farm will feed five thousand
I should worry about that too

Fencing

You always tell me
take one day at a time
two days of laundry
week's worth of weeding
month of payments behind
one day is not enough

Not enough time to pick beans
wash walls, prune perennials
need to make a good meal
clear the table, set china
silverware and paper serviettes

Instead, you and I share a bag lunch
beneath the poplars
dreams embedded in dust
finances planted in this soil
our lives interwoven
wild grass and river water

Here we hammer out life
one nail at a time
string barbwire post to post
each strand extended, miles
walking side by side
not much spoken, odd smile
so many decisions
made without words

And tomorrow
have to wash clothes
clean the bathroom basin

iron your cotton shirts
we'll argue about money
lifting the toilet seat
socks under the bed

You'll tell me, take one day at a time
and I'll tell you, tomorrow
we need to go fencing

Shut Down

These days no longer hold daisies, hot soup
warm buns, a killing frost, *what do I do now?*

Without soil and sod, whiskey barrels
full of nasturtiums and wild ivy
a wanderlust of living morning to midnight
drinking the land dry, pulling hurry root
and gather-me-bones into proper alignment, *shut down!*

Warns the winter solstice, her darkness a quilt
stitched — slow threads and paisley patches
on the edge of a caramel sun

Relax, says my mother on the phone, *you people*
just don't know how to relax

Coyote Dreams

November dying down, the horse has quickened his step
Saddle up! scour ragged edges, an ice cold prairie
abandon the greater herd for a weaker few

And sleep evades, elusive as the snow moon
her frozen promise won't let me forget
what about the strays?

Perhaps entangled in the willows, swallowed by the bog
we search with all the daylight we can gather
seize hope within the circle of the sun
only a few scattered bones

I dream December, a distressed sun
something of an opiate origami unfolds, bedded down
a thousand cattle sleep, border the outskirts of insomnia
infectious billow of steam rising from warm bodies
peace offering for tomorrow's sundogs

Tomorrow won't wait, naturally seasoned
hoar frost and reed canary tango with the winter solstice
her quarter moon shadow-dances, makes love
with aurora borealis, while slough-beds slumber and
I mourn the carcass in the cattails, the slow death of coyote
dreams

Ain't Gambling

Viva Las Vegas!
we're headed south
our boots and jeans
hat and kickers, off to the NFR

First time
never left the farm, too busy
cutting hay, too busy calving cows
too busy

This time
straight to Nevada
bunk down at Caesar's Palace
Excalibur, the Bellagio
ride bareback through Eldorado Canyon
kick it up at the NFR

What's that you say?
Aren't we going to gamble?

Nope
gambled all our lives
weather, trade barriers, politics
lifetime of Russian Roulette
barely breaking even

Nope, ain't gambling
just gonna stroll the Vegas strip

"NFR — National Finals Rodeo"

Daydreamer

Another day of sunshine, warm winds
if only I were an urban dweller
I'd whip up to Emma Lake
lie stranded in sand
soak up the sun
dream summer dreams

but

I am a farmer's wife
married to a tractor seat
hands black as the steering wheel itself
pilot me to exotic destinations
Caribbean seas, Jamaican islands
Hawaiian beaches, travelled many lands
pulling a set of hay rakes behind me

Here

On this land there are no hills, no trees
brown earthen slough-beds are vulnerable
barren ballroom where dirt devils
whirl and twirl invisibly, waltz into the porch
through my kitchen, leave silt and sand
on worn-out window frames, faded velvet drapes

Here there are no frills, no fancy tea trays
brown tweed chairs full of conversation
clutter space, fill days

Here I cook butterfly soup, seven-step pudding
polka steaks on the barbeque
slow dance the night brew with you

New Dog Dumb

A dog's decade crippled your speed
hampered vision, stole your ear
no longer able to work, I left you behind
an ornament for the front porch

Still you listen for my call *come by — way to me*
eager to nip heel and hoof
trolley back and forth behind the herd

Somewhere you smell the chase, taste grit
this grit between my teeth, I curse without you

Your whimpers lost to an unyielding wind
I choke dust, this new dog dumb, snotty bunch wild
pounds the spirited edge of your breakwater
crashes through my garden gate

Curse-Me-Not-Ditty

Something about an August evening
on the front porch swing while crickets sing
green leaves dance to night breezes
watching sunbeams hang on forever

Something about wanting to dance
you and I through meadow brome
seven step a coyotes call, tap buttercup gullies
swing back-forty rendezvous or nothing at all

Something about something
when nothing else matters
than having you serenade me in the calving barn
curse-me-not-ditty, get down and gritty
cuddle me when the sun has gone

ANCHORED

Warning!

Wild goose spoke from the northern sky
haunted the September sun
cool October nights
winter breath into womb
Warning! November came early
barley under snow, full belly moon
we'll harvest next season
paint cornflower blue
buy bottles and diapers
more peas and potatoes
plant one row or two

Warning! baby on board
strapped in the three ton
arrow root and apple juice
barley express tired
singing midnight blues
running low on diesel, diapers
last bit of daylight
dry winds
no dew
no stopping
shhh, don't cry baby
both of us are strong

Stubborn Words

You were born in the spring
with the Simmental and Shorthorn
laid in a manger, guarded by the dog
while we pulled calves, hard labour season
each one relived second breath

You grew up in the corral
product of Shellrose Stock Farm
counted cows and calves and bulls
recounted again and again
knew each one by number, their temperament
foul-ass names

Never had a chance for good language
rehearsal everyday
fine-tuned your father's phrases
didn't know enough to leave it in the cow pen
slipped up and told me, "you're full of shit"

Out came the cayenne and red pepper
liquid ivory, bitter green zest
washed and flushed your mouth for days
strong stubborn words — shit-stained

Children are what we teach them
your father taught you well

Sandbox Farm

Your fences are fine
unswerving line of popsicle sticks
with polished glass marbles
in blues, yellow, milky reds
all of course, a herd of longhorns
foraging on caragana leaf
sandy fields cultivated clean
never need weeding

Your hum diddle dum
filters the kitchen window
giddy up, giddy up, giddy up damn cows

Why couldn't farming be this simple
when you are grown

Who Killed the Ducks?

Was it you and your cousins tiptoed into the barn
bag of Quaker Oats, quart sealer of water
for Daffy and Doodle, grandpa's new baby ducks?

Held them like china, caressed downy wings
under your coat, quibbled away sound asleep

Was it you and your cousins in red rubber boots
green willow whips, snuck to the coop, ready to run?

Grandpa's old ducks flapping and quacking
boys yelling and screaming till someone gave in
or the ducks all played dead

It was you, quiet at grandma's table, fresh buns and butter
polite please and thank you, asked to be excused
ready for home, ready to flee, before grandpa came in
yelling, *who killed the ducks?*

Months later, your confession
how you chased them around that pen
rodeo like none other, each one collapsing
bodies strewn among chickens with strong hearts

Never meant this death, ten white Muscovy
their silence welling inside, day's later bursting your seams
I killed the ducks grandpa!

Christmas Goose

Should not have told you
how Billy and I set decoys and corn blinds
just before dusk on One Mile Creek
frozen hulls whispering, *warning, warning*
stagnant waters in the bottom of our boots
toes cold, blood hot, waiting for the geese

It set you to dreaming
goose and gander in our own back slough
faithful every year, silken-sky cry
good part of three seasons
Drove you to wanting the goose in my oven
a taste for yourself, a Christmas feast of old

With the shotgun and little brother
you bellied through cattails, rotten reed canary
waited like Setter dogs in the mud
late September sky, far away cry
getting closer and closer
every nerve coiled, closer and closer
you sprang from the muck, blasted the flock
she fell gray sky, dead centre
middle of the slough

Stripped down to britches you waded
cold water, hot blood
your goose bumps big as boiled eggs
wouldn't leave your Christmas goose
but neither would her mate
you fought him off with red willow
hauled her to shore

He left, not without voice
desolation over her death haunting
hurried you along skin and blood
ears covered, little brother dragging
the dead bird in a frenzy

Together we plucked her in the bush
clean shot, neck wound
the breasts would be good
but it wasn't what you thought
her warmth slipped into that pale night
his cry there till late November

December stuffed with celery, dried sage
slow cooked for hours
she was tough, leathery, bitter
chucked for nothing
ate whipped potatoes without gravy

That night, an army of stars laid blame
geese, guns, her carcass in the snow
next year, the skies would be silent

We are Campers

Away from the farm we pitch a tent
on the shore of Greenwater Lake
clothed in flannel pyjamas, wool socks
huddle close, listen to sleepy water at the shoreline
while night air dampens, cool skin

Children wedged between, are still
they speak in strained whispers, want to go home
away from overgrown shadows
mass of mosquitoes
they hate the back-bush biffy, toast on a stick
wonder why we have to stay

We stay, because it took three weeks
convincing their father
and two days to pack
and thirty-five dollars for the campsite

This night, we are campers
swallowed in darkness sleeping under a starry sky

Tomorrow, we'll go home and pick peas

Spring Ritual

Sit with you in a field of gophers
watch you shine the barrel
your father's twenty-two
on the sleeve of your red plaid shirt
admiring the gun for what it is
not for what it does

We watch brown heads bob in a sea of clover
your shot is good
only for salvation of winter feed
you pray each one goes to heaven

Consolation

Told you he was not a pet
not to get attached
promised me you wouldn't
he's just a brown steer mother
stupid brown steer, that's all

So why did you call him Pete, pat his head
tell him what a fine steer he was
you were diligent with feed and water
groomed his hair, trimmed his hooves
insisted he hold his head high
worked his feet with a showman stick
walked him everyday

4-H day came
you were up early in stiff blue jeans
loading supplies, you headed to town
with that stupid brown steer
he showed real well, third in class
you gave him a hug, extra bit of hay

At sale time, watery eyes, *get in line!*
bitter parade of steers
to noisy sale ring, eager buyers
you held his halter tight, *sold!*
dollar twenty five a pound
they loaded him on semi-trailer number two

On the way home a few sniffles
unwanted journey to an empty pen
in consolation, I told you about steer heaven
how much fun he'd have

playing ball with steer friends
munching corn chips, slurping barley pop
running free in green pastures
never being alone or sick or hungry

He'll always remember you, smart steers are like that

Sweetheart Supper

Grandmas and grandpas
moms and dads
aunts and uncles
neighbours and friends
all crowd in, small country hall
4-H fund-raiser

Take a seat, we'll serve
hip of beef
whipped potatoes
homemade hot rolls
more coleslaw please
cheese cake
and black coffee
a good meal
for good company

Lights down low
entertainment commences
cloggers from Canwood
hip hop and solos
crazy skits and cowboy poetry
Yee Haw, we've got a wild one
appetite for excitement, *bring on the auction*

Bids will be brisk
Brianne's brittle goes for a hundred
coffee can birdhouse, forty-five
Death by Chocolate, one hundred eighteen
all in -- all done
no one goes home hungry . . . *Sold!*

Searching

You waited all night checking hour to hour
as only a good herdsman does
at three AM you broke the water bag
four pushes, slight pull, back off, *Milly*

Together, huddled behind bales of straw
we watched her mother nuzzle with roughened tongue
the smell of birth hung heavy

It was time who whispered, *something wrong*
no fight to work wobbly legs, no eagerness
to suckle your finger, the teat
and winter at the barn door, icy fingers
craving her warmth

Your father spoke sternly, *leave it be*
as nature will have it, you know what will happen
we've been through this too many times

There was time for Pickles, time for Pinky
desperate eyes pleaded, time for Milly

I ignored the truth, bundled her up
in old floral quilts fresh with the smell of javex
strapped onto a wooden sleigh

We pulled her through the chill, your chatter
into the porch, a corner of the kitchen
laid her on a blue braided mat, heat lamp overhead

Again you waited and watched
her premature body, soft brown muzzle
heart beat flutter under bone and skin
searching for something that would never be found

Anchored

Should have known farm in your blood
seasons of sowing and reaping, of birth
and death . . . acceptance when that first calf
slipped away in the crook of your arms
and tears allowed your feelings so little
wouldn't meet your father's eyes, this one not meant to be

You've grown as the maple at the corner
planted when you were three, now taller than all of us
roots firmly fastened, anchored six feet deep

Your father's words
this black soil grows good crops
no guarantee, one year feast maybe next one famine
best you go to school and get a job

Your words
not a chance, spring seeding, summer silage, winter calving
you'll need another hand on this farm, you always told me
two heads are better than one, that's what you said dad
two heads are better than one

My words
let him stay

Friday Night Calls

It’s those Friday night calls to the farm
buddies from town, work week finished
time to party, get drunk, whoop it up

Not as before, school days asleep
paying the girl next to you
for study notes, half-assed essay
running wild all weekend
my dreading everyone

I tell them you’re busy with calving
time swallowed in grain dust and after birth
awakening to life as a full-fledged farmer

Alcohol won’t do you any good
adrenaline overdose to manage this farm
please your father, is wearing thin

It’s no, he’s staying home, going to bed

He’ll be angry tonight
weary eyes thankful tomorrow

Edge of Broke

Wasn't ready for tea parties and tears
how you grew through my fingers into freckles, 4-H calves
men's wranglers, the John Deere 4840
watched you spread like wildfire, burning for top showman
as your grandfather was

Wasn't ready for beer parties and broken hearts
how I became nothing more than a maid
mending jeans, washing clothes, cooking steaks
listening to your crap, not saying a word

Wasn't ready when you told me, *I'm through with this shit*
late nights brutal, on the edge of broke
this fence needs mending, dad's right
this business won't work, farming five days a week
drinking Pilsner for two, hung-over for three
I'm ready for this farm . . . hope it's ready for me

Fighting Words

When the moon slides on the edge of midnight
she waits for me, a promise light
cracks winter air, harvesting the dark
narrow trail within good sight
Did she know this winter's fate?

Been two months since the accident
short days, very little time for self-pity
calving full-steam ahead — don't set the clock

For I've become nocturnal, share the long
cold nights with a snowy owl and three barn cats
sit with the darkness, her warmth of birthing
erasing any uncertainty, I will get through this

A girl of chickadee mornings and quiet evenings
could never have embraced such darkness
but the boys have worked more than their fair share
and you in a wheelchair disgruntled with healing
wonder why we take so long, *all damn day!*

Fighting words! Does experience need to remind you?
tractors, feed wagons and humans don't
operate well in forty below, we are one good man short!

What is love anyway?

I say it's born, an infant held close
to his mother's breast
two young lovers beneath an opal moon
sweet clover wrapped, raw skin
everyone has an opinion

Perhaps love found you
when you fed the old dog with a crippled hip
gave him fresh bread, your leftovers
kept the young pup away

When you brought me the bird
with a broken neck, still breathing
someone had to end this agony
not you

And now today you've quit work
taken on your father's farm
his crushed hip, smashed ribs
battle lost with a power take-off
and from a window he watches you
fill the feed wagon, roll grain
clean the calving barn by hand

He can see your inexperience
tells you how to fix the alternator
when to sell in the market
but he can't tell you that he loves you
it has never been said
trapped in the red willow of his heart
but we all know - it's love

Someday for Me

Tell me the old, old story
when you were a boy, grandfather
walked four miles to school
used a slate and chalk
ate lunch from a maple syrup can

Tell me about your britches
top leather boots, same tartan shirt
starched, pressed each day
the jackknife in your pocket
to whittle willow fish poles

Tell me about trapping gophers
forty tails carved, recounted
stuffed into a tobacco can
sold for two cents each
so you could buy black licorice pipes

And don't forget Jack and Ginger
how they pulled the plow
cut this land, you behind
leathered reins and a sisal whip
breaking new ground for you
someday for me

Holding On

February Poems

February 9

Here's to the wind-chill all minus forty-eight of it
harsher yet, late night hours pulling warm, wet calves
pulling ourselves from warm, dry beds
layered a foot deep

She licks placenta nudges the calf, *get up*
and suck, but how when you're wet and cold
veins pumping bloody icicles to a tepid heart
kicking wind from her teats, all wrong
off-season

We are guilty, fight nature, each other
the cost, allow winter between us
snow, two feet deep, fail to unthaw, inch by inch
words freezing until we become icebergs, emotional glaciers
stare at each other with cold eyes

February 11

Sitting at the window, a Hungarian partridge
from beneath the spruce boughs skitters across the yard
to high bush cranberries hanging dead-weight
on brittle branches

She jumps for the limb, stretching
neck arched for just one berry, minutes into half hours
she jumps for berries, for food, for life

It's noon, in for a bite home now on stress leave
a son with pericarditis, or as he puts it
ticker under my lift tit not working so well

Unable to lift, he belts out the orders in a kind fashion
much rather be doing the chores himself

I'm not nearly his replacement, but I clean the barn
each forkful much heavier than five years ago
when we took on the farm, his father in the hospital

Five years older, five more forkfuls thrown into
the manure wagon, short jerky strides, load after load
minutes into hours until it's clean

The partridge has taken five berries, finished
for this day and for a moment she peers through the window
as if to say, *why do you do this?*

February 13

Thinking winters are getting longer and harder
almost unbearable

Don't want to live here anymore
can't bear forty below down my spine
watching hump-back cows crawl to their feed
brittle bones, blood-blue veins

Want to move to Maple Creek
charted the temperature for three years
ten to fifteen degrees warmer, very little snow

But you've always had an excuse, too much wind
edge of drought, rough and rocky and
rolling and free spirited where cattle graze
stock run tough on prairie wool and before
you know it

You want to leave too, but your Scotch bones
won't tolerate change and your progeny
won't hear nothing of it, *don't do it dad*
we're part of this North, clear cut
as the pristine lakes themselves, *don't do it dad*

Alone, wanting to leave the only home I've known
since eighteen, wanting to leave the snow, the cold
and calving and feeding and day after day B.S.
that goes on in this so-called cattle business

Wanting sand and sun, soft kisses, hot tacos
hot nights, cool ocean breezes, you, me and a beach
bikini love song . . . maybe we should move to Mexico

February 14

In the barn, you tell me
don't leave so much crap in the aisle
when you carry, don't take a big load
smaller piles, more trips, too much shit already
and on and on we go

There are no women I know
whose weekends are tied up in manure
hauling two-fold from a stinking barn
forkful after forkful, slime-wet straw
second-day afterbirth

No women I know would skin dead calves
with a rusty utility knife
placenta still sticky, edges of my hands
tied around a twin needing a mother

Not many women would do this
if you want my help, shovel and shut up!

February 17

The barn is quiet, calving calmed to a couple of newborns
an orphaned calf and a crippled twin vacate this space

Two days old, this crippled twin
whose mother stepped on his back, can't walk
he's pulled from the pen without evening nursing

We feed him replacer, he struggles with the hard
rubber nipple, only hours ago he nursed
his mother's soft teat, warm spray of milk rippling his nose

As he drinks, I can't help wonder what will happen
what really should be done with this calf?

This calf is your project, you feed him
and move him and ultimately deal with his death

But I know you can't do away with him any more
than I can, and our son tells us, *your hearts are good*
sometimes, too good

This day a crippled twin and orphan have each other
you and I consider the options, consensus agreed
my son knows it will all end in bloodshed

February 23

Time to feed the calves, two portion milk
and one water for the crippled twin, one week old
and still with us, eager to win back his legs

Don't think I've seen a calf with such a ton of heart
therapy three times a day, he's flipped every hour
and rubbed down with liniment

My son tells me,
this calf, just like the old guy in the hospital
I roomed with, shattered hip, great guy Ed
been flipped every three hours, two months now

Let's call him Ed

And when we name a calf, it's hard to let go
we need all forces to see him through
at whose cost, your father says, *don't let him suffer*

February 25

Today's been wild and sad, cleaning barns
unthawing water bowls, thirsty cows crowd and fight
not one ounce of order, stupid animals

Haven't had a wild cow for some time
but this one's an all-star, bought sight unseen
her calf too big, needs a pull
in and out of the barn, who's chasing who

I'm not getting in with her and if you do
you're on your own

But I'm ready with a steel bar, iron wits
I bang and clang, scream, curse and holler
through her defences, somehow in the chute
call the vet, *Could you come calve this T-Rex?*

He pulls on the edge of uncertainty
big, black calf, crazy heifer, should have
been a caesarean, too much stress
I close the door and leave

Find Ed, crippled twin, basking in
the last minutes of daylight
back legs limp and stiff, Ed standing tall
as if to say . . . *I will mend*

The vet gives no hope, plainly stated
try if you want, his back legs are dead
I let Ed slip gentle into the straw
sun-yellow sadness, cold chill coming on
feed him a double portion, extra pillow of hay

Part of this day creeps into the night
stiff joints, ring finger two sizes larger
hangnail weepy, sober thoughts of Ed
stir beneath my pillow, cow angels in the morning

February 26

Finally the sun peeks through an east window
squeak of light just before eight, spring twinkle
something of warmth and life, renewal

My son, how happy, echocardiogram
shows normal heart function
back to work as usual, no more
cursing and coaching from the fence line

You summon my pitchfork,
muscles bulge and ripple, claim back this farm
with both hands and four words

Mother, go make dinner

February, 30

> *Oh farmer's excessively fortunate, if only they recognized their blessings!* — Virgil

Been home three tough weeks, cold and wind
hundred and fifty calves brought into existence
but the toughest, dealing with life and death
holding onto each other's words, holding on
for each other

Should be happy, going back to work
somehow tied in a knot, leaving the men
this farm, and if they knew how I felt
they'd truly be insulted, can't run the outfit without me

But that's not it, I've settled back into barley straw
long hours of winter air, same day routine
enjoy lunch together, quiet minutes of
sunshine at the dining room table
warm, weak coffee, whole wheat toast

Been good wearing toque hair, comfortable
in coveralls, barn boots, no make-up or
nail polish, no fuss and mess with flat irons,
ribbon curls, polyester slacks, acrylic sweaters

Raw and chaffed as the winter air, I'm tired
arms and wrists ache, lifting, shovelling, pulling
and praying for warmer weather, healing hearts

thank you Jesus

Going back to work
black jeans, white blouse, pink boots
soft-shaded smile, farm heavy heart

Trust

This night — the snow moon is welcome, a blazing
ball of orange, she quietly emerges from an earthly womb
a sure reminder that my watch is weeks overdue

At midnight, her translucent white speaks soft mercies
the low breath and moans of calving, spiritual notations
morning's first hymn

I've come to accept my place in this birthing barn
where new life reminds me of the good shepherd
all I need to do is check — *trust* — sleep, inevitably
the rest will look after itself

First Snow

Suddenly
winter clouds
woven blue-gray
silvery stars
into shadowy silence
fence posts white
farmyard quiet

breathe!

        breathe!

                breathe!